At the Speed of God

Another small book of a poet's prayers

Sister Mary Grace, DMML

i

Published by the Daughters of Mary,
Mother of Healing Love
www.motherofhealinglove.org
Rochester, NH
USA

ISBN 978-0-9973546-1-4

Printed in the United States of America

Almighty God
thank You

for sorrow and joy,
and all that lies between.

Table of Contents

A Dime for Your Time

What if Jesus showed up right now!
Not for judgement, for a moment with
the scrambled eggs, the last load of laundry,
the dime you found on the floor.

What if He didn't say a word,
but you knew He was with you;
because the eggs tasted really, really good
even though you hadn't changed the recipe,
the oil, the skillet, the plate, the fork,
or the kind of egg;
and the laundry just seemed to
wash and dry and fold itself
in record time with uncommon ease;

and the dime snapped to its edge
when you put it on the desk,
as if it were a soldier
immediately obedient to its commander.
You would have expected it to lie flat
on its head or its tail,
because that's what dimes and other coins
always do.
When you want them to stand on edge,
they wobble and fall flat,
so it isn't worth your patience or your effort;

1

but this dime had something to say
with the help of the Word.
You stared and smiled and took a picture
of this out-of-the-ordinary dime
to text to your best friend;
but what would you text?
Would you say it was uncanny
how it seemed to leave your hand
and stand and remain on its edge,
even after you'd left the room
and returned and found it unchanged?
Would you mention Jesus,
that He came to mind,
as if He were keeping that dime on its edge
with a thought of His Heart?
Even if you didn't mention His Name,
Jesus would still be
on your mind and in your soul;
and you'd go through the rest of the day smiling,
that dime edged in your head;
laughing, when you thought of Him thinking of
you,
giving you a moment with Him;
thinking how little a thing He'd done, just for
you,
to bring you to the edge of joy;
but that's how He is.
Jesus just wants time with us.

August

On her last birthday she turned sixty,
and she remembered and spoke about
her trips to Europe with Gloria, her best friend.
Rome was her favorite,
because it reminded her of where she would be,
some day...

She saw Papa from a distance, and he blessed
her.
It didn't matter that he couldn't see her.
God was pleased that she was there, looking for
Him;
and He allowed Papa's words to soak her soul
like a long, cool drink for her thirst.
She was refreshed and joyful
and looking forward to 61,
just months away from walking away
from the work she'd done
since she was a twenty-something, wife and
mom;
but God had a different plan...

She never saw sixty-one.
She saw the One
Who gave her sixty years
to find Him where He'd always been

waiting in her heart.

Blessing Cup

No one heard her last breath
in the rooms that she kept
tidy and white like the light
surrounding her now.

They would not let me near her,
as if I could disturb her.

She has ceased to need
the garments she had made
and the dreams she had prayed
at Jesus' feet...
except one.

She had hoped that before she died
her daughters would realize
God is closer than the phone;
that they are never alone in their misery,
nor lost in their history.

She proved that white is not a color
but a state that penetrates a soul
once grace soaks and soothes and saves us.
Her daughters will see, as will we,
that death has neither diminished nor

extinguished
who God created her to be.
Prayer is the bridge connecting us,
keeping us, protecting us
from the harness of despair.
Hope is our portion of grace.

Blue Hope

She keeps her pain
locked tight in a box
buried at the base of Blue Hope.

We don't approach Blue Hope
because of that box.
We know it's there;
but we don't speak
about the box,
or the body in it.

He was all she had;
not quite three,
blue eyes like his dad,
curly hair like hers;
a smile to a giggle to a laugh
that kept us smiling
most of the day and into the night,
when we'd shut our eyes tight
against ever losing that little piece of him.

His smiles, his giggles, and his laughter
were free and plenty,
and he was generous with his gifts.
He climbed Blue Hope every day,

leaving his mom and his dad
in the wake of his speed, his energy and his joy.

After the headaches began,
he could not convince his body to continue;
but his spirit reached the summit
faster and more often
than he ever could with his feet.
He laughed when he said that to his mom and
his dad,
just before he closed his eyes the last time.
She had heard his whispered conversations with
his pals,
Saint Michael, his guardian angel and the
Blessed Mother.
He never complained about the pain.
He just explained and described it
as well as any almost-three-year-old would.

A battle in his head, he would say.
But it was okay because Saint Michael and his
guardian angel,
and the Blessed Mother were with him.
Not to fret, he would say to his mom.
Not to fret.
And she believed him and didn't worry.
Not too much anyway.
The doctors said their powerful drugs would
ease the hurt;

but he knew Jesus would give him what he
needed
to grow a heart as big as His.

She knew when she walked in his room
that Jesus was holding him now;
that Jesus would walk with him
up and down the mountain
with Saint Michael and his guardian angel,
and the Blessed Mother:
the Blue Hope.

Branches Against Blue

Stripped
of their clothing and colors,
they can only wait
for His breeze
to move them slightly,
or with ferocity,
or not at all.
They have
no thoughts,
no desires;
just obedience
against His constancy of sky.

Candidate

Food
should be
delicious,
satisfying
and digestible
with zero discomfort.
Three-ingredient, bite-sized
shortbread cookies get my vote for
every meal, since, with a nod from God,
they could become the new desert manna.

Coins Not Required

If you're thinking
money is the great eraser
of pain and poverty and injustice and...
you're mistaken.
You've been taken
into the chamber of deceit.
Retreat
from that abode!
I realize
you must decide
for yourself
what you will take
from the shelf of life,
but please consider this:
the One Who made and keeps
the Atlantic and Pacific,
Kilimanjaro,
maple trees and birch trees,
magnolia blossoms,
sunrise, sunset, snowflakes,
jasmine, Felix, and you,
is not charging you rent.
He just wants your time spent
with Him.

Command Performance

Imagine,
quitting the sphere
of all you hold dear...
family, friends, possessions,
obsessions, digressions,
distractions, attractions;
regrets, misgivings,
sin...
to follow God,
to allow God
to subtract
your thoughts,
your desires,
your dreams
until you exit stage left
to the balcony seat beside Him,
to see His life played out through you.

Companion

She walked down the aisle holding her mother's
hand,
looking up at her at every other step.
She was too big to be carried now.
She carried herself to the priest
placing Jesus in every soul.
She saw Jesus just as she saw her mother.
And she thought it odd that some
didn't seem to recognize Him
or dismissed Him as just another to-do.
She wanted to linger and watch each one receive
Him.
But her mother tugged her gently,
pulling her away from Jesus
and toward Him at the same time;
because Jesus is where we've been
and where we're going,
and where we want to be.

Constant

Most mornings, the ache wakes me;
breaks the peace into pieces I must gather
along the path of the day.

Peace is the path I must uncover.
It is narrow and uninviting
to the undiscerning eye,
the frantic heart focused on the pain.

Peace is the pain,
unrestrained and unaware of its
assistance in keeping me
faithful, purposeful.

I persist in my pursuit of the Irresistible:
Jesus,
Whose perfect peace on the cross
never shatters,
ever gathers each piece of my peace.

Consumed

Anita Abigail left her o in the chapel
this morning after Mass.
If she had seen it beneath the kneelers,
she would have placed it in her mouth
and let it rest on her tongue
as if it were the finest, sweetest, most delicious
morsel ever.

She was new enough to the world of o
to know that each one was not to be
rushed down the throat, but savored.

If the opening in the center of the o could speak,
it would thank Anita Abigail
for allowing it to become part of her;

unlike the Eucharistic Jesus,
Whom we take into our hearts
with thanksgiving to God
for allowing Jesus to consume us.

Curtis

He had not planned to navigate his days
on crutches or in a wheelchair.
His choice was football:
playing it, watching it;
teaching his sons to be the best players of the
game,
like he was.
His wife was his number one fan.
She always was.
Still?
He wouldn't ask.
What if she were looking for a way out?
Had he no faith in her?
Had he faith at all? Ever?
He needed to believe in the God Who made
him,
Who kept him in a body he could no longer use
as he chose.
His wife told him to pray.
His mother told him to pray.
His aunt, who'd been a nun
longer than he'd been in the flesh,
told him the only way he'd make it through this
trial
was to pray without taking a breath.
He didn't know how.

17

He didn't believe
there could be anything beyond this
slow motion slide down a mountain he never
climbed.
The ground just dropped out from under him;
and his fingers bled as he snatched at rocks,
holding on as long as he could
to avoid the inevitable abyss.
His aunt said prayer is letting go,
letting the Lord keep him from despair;
letting his heart inform his reason
that reason has no place on this particular path;
that this is the heart's journey
into the Heart of Jesus.
He needed that kind of faith.
He wanted that kind of faith.
His aunt told him the story of Abraham and
Isaac on the mountain;
told him to read it every day, nine times a day or
more,
for forty-five days or more,
until the story made its home in his soul,
constantly feeding him like breath.
From there, the Lord God would take him
deep into a faith that would so overwhelm him
that his body would understand and respond
in seemingly impossible ways;
that life, with or without legs that worked in the
expected way,
would no longer matter.

What matters is God:
His constancy,
His immediacy,
His perfect plan.

Delores

For a moment, I was in Texas,
Prosper, Texas,
standing in the driveway of the red brick house
where she would have moved,
had she lived.
The sun was high and hot,
and her dog had found a patch of shade
on the lawn near her chair,
the one she'd bought at the Kmart
before it closed.
"Five bucks," she'd said,
with her tall glass of ice tea in her hand.

I sat in her chair and stared at Red,
asleep on the grass,
probably dreaming of her;
picturing her with Jesus, still sipping her tea,

telling Jesus about her five-dollar chair;
what a deal it was,
how comfortable it was,
how she was glad it was pink;

because pink is the color of the sky
when you look at it just right,

just before sunrise;
just before you breathe
your last breath.

Desperation

I am done
with every fast, every novena,
every memorized prayer;
not because they're not working,
but because they're not working fast enough for
me.
That's what I tell myself
and my spiritual director.

I pray, Father, but nothing is changing!
Everything is getting worse!

Nothing, everything…
these extremes are important.
They remind me
that I have closed every door, every window
to the Good God;
and I've drawn the shades
so I can draw myself up into a ball
in a corner in the dark.

That's when Father Rah Rah
noses into my nose dive and says,
"Tongues."
I roll my eyes;

but then I realize, I've got nothing to lose.
So I open my mouth and babble on
like I used to do with my best friend when we
were kids,
pretending to be fluent in French or Swahili;
and I realize, it is another language leaving my
lips;
taking me to places I never thought I could go in
the flesh.

I have the Ear of God,
because He's giving me the words I couldn't
give Him;
the words He wants to hear from me with my
voice,
the voice He gave me
to praise Him,
to worship Him,
to give all to Him;
because He's desperate for me too.

Dieffenbachia & Company

In a lineup by a window,
His green and growing things
have my attention
with no wordy mention
of their intention
to bask in every ray
that warms and lights the day.
They merely stand in silence,
in perfect reliance
upon God.

Some might think it odd
that I hear their silent prayer,
write it off as just the air;
but words need not be said
with ramblings from a head
too full of its own desires
to allow God to inspire
with ways and wonders too extravagant to hold.

Would God be so bold?
Indeed, for He is Lord,
and He desires sweet accord
among His many creatures.

Our features are no random quirks.
He knows and ascertains what works.
Each green and growing plant
reminds me that I can't
be the keeper of my soul.
I accept His stole of grace,
hasten to His Pace,
and praise and thank Him all my days
for His glorious and giving ways.

Done

Three priests in the church
ponder the life of spent flames
from broken candles.

Flow

Off-
putting,
this sunset
bout of sadness
replacing gladness,
until sleep silences
thoughts and feelings like a drape
commanding motionless moments
of unrelenting focus on God,
irresistible in His mighty glance.

Flutter Club

They seemed unaware of me
on the sidewalk,
as they hovered near each other,
doing their best to imitate hummingbirds.
Their bodies and their wings
were much too big,
but they fluttered on
for themselves and for each other
on the railing of the porch
of the house in disrepair.

Perhaps
its occupant would imitate their gaiety
and set aside his grief long enough
to repair and replace
and mend the broken-hearted house
that longed to be aflutter again;
as in the days of Faith,
who seemed to glide
through each room and hall
for him who had lived his life for her.

Perhaps
he would notice the fragrance
of her prayers for him
and rise from his way of pain,
imitating her way
of joy and trust in God.

Insistent in their way
of celebration,
hesitation is not their say.
Their day is too short to carry agony.
Agony will not allow them to flutter.
Flutter they must against the leaves of death,
which give them reason and wings to celebrate.

Flyers

He
wanted
a son who
would fly the kite
he had made the night
his wife told him about
their child in her womb; but he
left the womb, took a breath, and left
with Jesus, Who flies the kite with him
each night in his mom's and dad's seamless
dreams.

Forecast

Storm
warnings
will not stay
the Hand of God
upon each task He
gives me to accomplish.
His mighty Arm upholds me.
His is the Breath that allows me
without pause or trepidation to
leave all calculations to Christ Jesus.

Grand Design

Our reduction from eight to seven
was executed in Heaven
without consultation from me,
for I am not He.

I had prayed and been waylaid
by His Masterpiece.
He would not cease.

I pleaded.
Others interceded;
but He would hear none of it.
He wanted me to sit
in obedience to Him,
despite the dim
pictures in my head.
Fitfully I lay in dread
of each day that He had painted,
so tainted was my soul.

In time, He brought me to a place
where I imagined His Face
was always taking me in,

no matter the gravity of my sin;
He chose to hold me in His glance,
slice me through with His own lance;
to open my heart to His Way,
to rescue me without delay.

He knows His plan for me:
freedom from all I need not be.

Gratitude

Gratitude is an attitude,
a voice that makes a choice
to be kind,
whatever the bind
that tugs at the heart
to abandon its part
in God's army.

Fierce is the battle to pierce the soul
making its way to the Eternal Day.

No need to choose fear,
Almighty God is here!
The evil one has lost.
Jesus picked up the cost
with His life and with His death.
Thank God with every breath!

Head to head

You used to give me
an image of You and me
on the Face of the Host
in the monstrance.
I haven't seen that in a long time,
not since the chapel
at Immaculate Heart.
Even there, in my last days,
You didn't show up.

That image wouldn't be
enough for me now;
still, it would be
no small kindness to see You and me
in that Head to head conversation,
neither of us saying a word;
but You knowing my every thought
before I even think it;
every joy, every sorrow,
before they overtake me;
and me allowing You
to overtake me.

Heaven

I had never seen a sparrow chasing a moth
in a duet of gray and white twirling toward the
sky;
until this morning, as I was chasing time
around an oval pavement.

As I approached, they abandoned their dance,
perhaps alarmed by my uninvited observation.
I had hoped to capture and share their private
conversation,
a rare moment I might never see again.
Without an image in the memory of my camera,
to support my telling the tale of this tiny piece
of God's fabulous glory,
the details will fade and succumb to the frailties
and limitations of my mind.

But God remembers what He gives me.
This is the measure of Heaven.
All the good that He gives me here,
all that is excellent and superb
and delightful and inspiring
and amazingly wonderful beyond words,

He keeps it all in the eternal space
of His unfathomable being:
every sparrow,
every moth,
every Atlantic and Pacific wave,
every setting and rising sun,
every sliver and fullness of moon.
every child who smiles and laughs with me,
every infant who sleeps secure in my arms…
Mercy erases the stuff that insists
 it is immune to my forgetful mind.

God's memory is a trinity.
With every event, every person, every place
He allows in the tiny space of my life in the
flesh,
He knows the before, the during, the after.
Each moment is as He ordains.
I will know I am Home with the Good God
Almighty
when I again see the moth and the sparrow.

This time, in such exquisite detail,
and for such an extravagance of time,
they will see me as a delightful friend
who is most welcome to the swirls of their
gaiety.

Hunger

Discomfort is my choice.
It is a necessary voice
reminding me that I
will die.

Daily I complain
about my aches, my pain;
but my decision to abstain
is so that I may attain
a fresh perspective on the reign
of Christ.

I long for my favorite food.
It improves my mood.
Without it I brood
to the point of becoming rude.

I would be at my best
if I could once more rest

in a house of my own,
all alone;

with the exception of a cat
who would purr instead of chat.
I remember that.

Such thinking makes me wonder
if I have made a blunder.
Perhaps God would have sent His thunder
to confirm that my choice was under
His command.

But whatever I choose,
God does not abandon me to the blues.
He sends His Mother,
no other will do.

Instep

"Let her be,"
He said, when they questioned me
about the food on my plate,
the curls in my hair,
the freckles on my face,
the style of my attire...
To silence Him, they let me be;
but the look they gave me
said they would resume
when He left the room.
He saw it too and said,
"Follow Me."
I smiled and left
and chose the path to His river,
its current swifter than stones and boulders
breaking from their ledge.
At the river's edge,
I poured my dismay
into His spray

of glory and might
evident in the river;
and I prayed they would follow
and see Him in the water
and sit long by the water
and praise Him
and, like the river, proclaim Him
Lord God Almighty!

Journey

One
hour
is too long
to spend driving
home after a day,
sitting and listening.
Minutes become months that
linger like listless, lost years
in chambers of cold molasses.
Uninterrupted, solitary
stillness, silence, and home are required.

Memory as Good as Presence

She remembers the moment
Jesus spoke to her.
There were others in the church
that Friday evening,
but no one else seemed to recognize
the Holy Spirit
speaking through the priest.

She set aside the printed words
of the Stations of the Cross,
asking herself,
"Who IS this guy?"
But she knew.
Stunned and bewildered,
she had no words within her
to offer a worthy thanksgiving
for the Father's incomparable gift.

For a time, God allowed her
to linger on the mountain top
of His Mystery and Majesty,
concealing His Mission
of Misery and Mercy
until His appointed time.

He had created her for this work,
knowing that she could
suffer what others would dismiss
as ill-fitting for even a fool.

In her wretched devastation,
she would long for the Holy Spirit
and look for Jesus,
tracing the etchings of Him:
the season, the day, the time,
the place, the priest;
the incomparable gift that she could open
as often as she needed
the Power of God the Father,
the Peace of God the Holy Spirit,
the Presence of God the Son, Jesus.

Momentary

Animosity's viscosity
suffocates the ill-prepared.
They reason that they
should be spared,
having led an exemplary life
of toil and sacrifice
totally free of vice,
by their own estimation.
So flawed is their summation
they do not recognize
His Eyes upon them.
"Who are you, sir?"
"I Am," He states,
leaving no room for debate.
Still their eyes are blind;
but He, with a smile, doesn't mind.
He is patient. He is kind.
In His mercy He gives us time
and predicaments
that only He can define
and unbind.
Ah, the meek shall inherit the earth.
The rest of us shall reek
of resentment and pettiness

and tantrums...
Still, He is patient,
He is kind.
He knows the moment
He will unbind
the strings of things in which we trusted.
He alone is to be trusted
and followed
and loved
and adored
and looked for
and listened to...
in every moment.
He is the Maker
and Master
of every moment.

Movement

Two
glasses
of water,
insufficient
to move quiche along
the lengthy path within,
were followed by other ones.
In the wake of their failure, I
listen: God's oboe of patient trust
moves me and all that remains within me.

Open

Sleep
allows
another
moment to pray,
uninterrupted
by the details of days
grown stale by routines that fail
to acknowledge the needs of those
who seek creativity, not boxed
scenarios that leave no room for God.

At the Speed of God

Heaven is the is-ness of God.
God is Father.
God is Son.
God is Holy Spirit.
God is Almighty.
God is with us always.
God is love.
God is patient.
God is kind.
God is mercy…
and we are in the midst of Him.
Our eyes cannot see His Face.
Our ears cannot hear His Voice.
But our hearts are not blind
to His Eyes,
nor deaf to His Words.
His Heart is ever tending our wounds.
Our hearts know
we are never without Him.
Absence is absent from His Nature.
How absurd
to think our prayers are ever unheard.
Indeed, they are heard and answered
before we even think them,
before we speak them;
before we determine that His particular speed

is not to our liking.
All of our tears are counted and kept.
They are the best prayers,
the best conversations with God.
Our sobs and salt water prepare us
for that moment when God gives us
the grace to surrender,
to ease into life at His speed.

Ordinary

He
had not been given a burning bush
or a tiny whispering sound.
If he had followed his father's example,
he would not have received
Jesus in the Eucharist;
but his mother was faithful,
and his father did not demand
that she join him
in his Mass abstinence.
The notion of him becoming a priest
was suggested by another;
and he, like his father,
did not object.

She
busied herself with the Church
in the devastation of her father's death.
In her grief,
the Lord God was there with her,
and loved her more
than she could love herself.
Later, when her husband
died too soon,
Jesus was still with her,
closer to her than she could imagine.

They
are disciples of the Good God Almighty,
Who astounds and delights
in extraordinary ways;
and in ordinary time,
He is in the going and the coming
and the doing of our ordinary days;
and in the faces and the ways
and the stories of ordinary people
who never leave us.

Our Lady of Sorrows

Agony entered,
and you entered
the Sacred Heart of your Son,
Jesus,
Whose death left you
not bereft,
but stouthearted
in doing the Father's will:
accepting,
surrendering,
trusting
that peace would empty itself
into the emptiness
of your Immaculate Heart,
that spaciousness of grace
none can fathom nor ignore,
but ceaselessly implore
your constant,
your fervent intercession.

Pack

Don't look back at what could have been,
had you sat tight in the company of your own
making.
This current undertaking,
this travesty as you see it,
is allowed by God,
is designed by God
to bring you Home to Him.

Admit that this is true,
and let it all go;
your worries, your fears,
the limiting loop in your head
that all is lost because of your
stupidly conceived and callously executed
calamities that you grieve.
Give it all to God.

Passenger

If I were in charge, this barge
would not be my transportation
to the next station:
but captain I am not;
consequently, my lot
is total trust;
even as the failed crust
of my disappointing pie
is all that eye can see.
I must forget about me
and focus on Him
Who knows my every whim.
He, my Blessed Savior, never fails me,
ever regales me,
with His amazing ways
in every breath of my days.
He died for me,
yet He remains with me:
present always,
calling me always
to embrace all of His Ways.
Every particle is an article
from Him and about Him.
No circumstance is dim
in the light of Him
Who knows all,

Who waits for us to call
His Name and proclaim:
Jesus is the Christ
of the wary,
the contrary,
the ordinary
the extraordinary...
Almighty Lord of ALL!

Perfectionist

He entered,
noticed the chairs,
tugged each a little here, a little there
until both front legs of every chair
touched the reasonably straight line in front of
them
in precisely the same manner.

Precision is his banner.
Every day progresses to his liking
when objects remain
where he places them,
when nothing unexpected or new
comes into his view.
People are not so easy.
They move.
They displace, replace,
vacillate, congregate,
segregate, integrate,
and express their distaste
for his exacting ways;
but he is learning to let go of his wishes,
recognizing that we are not dishes
to be scraped and rinsed and washed
and rinsed and dried and put away.

We live and move and have our being
in God, not in him,
but including him.

God is patient with His son.
God is in no way done
with His son.

Petition

Again,
salt water rises,
ready to fall.
I cannot stall
the obvious drip,
the quivering lip;
the breaking heart
that leaves no part
of me in doubt about
my need to plead my cause.
Lord God, give pause
to this suffocating dark.
Open my eyes to the mark
that declares I am Yours.
Open all the doors
I slam.

I Am,
convince me
You love me.
Use every tool
to bring the sorry fool
in me to my knees!
Please!

Pocketed

Her
small blue
pocketbook
waits in its place,
waiting for her to
take it in hand when she
ends her time in this tidy,
spacious place of eighteen windows
always watching, as the Atlantic
washes the pockets of pain in her book.

Poet

Poet, stow it
in your head and in your heart
and in your hands,
lest it leave without a hint
that it was ever present.

Poet, show it
in flowing ink upon a page,
that it may rage
like a tire loosed
from a broken car's demise.

Poet, know
it will not be heard
or understood by every soul.
In most, it will never break
itself or the soul.
New life will not begin;
but it will have achieved its end.
God's plan is perfect,
even in still birth.

Pray 3

Life in the prayer lane
is the way to abstain
from a life too full
of stuff that can pull
us away from God.

With just a nod
in His direction
we can resist the selection
of unholy choices
despite the voices
determined to mislead us.

It is best not to discuss
anything with anyone
who forsakes the Son.
Simply pray for salvation
for all in every nation,
and consider every event
as consistent with God's intent
to save every soul.

Let us assist God in His goal!
Let us pray

every day
in every way!

Pray 4

Prayer
must be like the air;
always sustaining,
ever pertaining

to the person with whom I am speaking,
to the answers I am seeking,
to the water that will not stop leaking
from my eyes.

Prayer's disguise
can put off most
who are unwilling to boast,
like Paul,
who allowed God to do all
through him.

Prayer takes us out on every limb,
lets us hang there for awhile
until we just have to smile
and admire
God,
Who does not perspire
at all.
He is always waiting for us to call

His Name,
to give up our game
of pretending we are self-sufficient
and admirably proficient
at whatever we choose to do.

But here's the point:
We are not in charge of this joint.
He is!
Every detail is His!
So let Him have His Way,
and listen to what He has to say
about the place He is preparing,
about not sparing
Jesus
for us.

Providence

You
give me
substantial
gifts that I have
never been able
to give myself. I thought
I had provided well for
myself. I was wrong. Forgive me.
Forgive my foolish adoration of myself.
Thank You, Lord God, for saving me from me.

Raccoon

He saw me
before I noticed him
near the top of a lean, sturdy tree.
His deep dark eyes looked into the brown
of mine, and we allowed wonder and delight
to silence any inkling of fright or flight.

Unthreatened, he resumed his work,
and I continued my walk,
grateful for the reminder
that God's creatures reflect His Features.

Realization

Not quite nine,
but too late to dine
on fish
or any other dish.

He insists.
She resists.
Confrontation ensues,
long overdue.

His voice rises.
She realizes
calm is required
in the midst of this fire;

but if this is prophesy,
she would be obliged to flee,
avoiding the inevitable fights
that would be the substance of their nights.

Her angel urges her to pray,
even though she knows not what to say;
but as God listens and feeds her heart,
she sees the rage depart.

And they, in His peace, understand

that they live not
at their command.
They will taste grace and thrive,
with God directing their lives.

Ride By

Bike
rider
called to me,
asked me to pray
for him. I said, "Pray
for me too." He looked me
in the eye as he peddled
by, opened his mouth and left me
with a word and his face in my heart;
a lingering, last word for me: "Amen."

Run

One
Audi
waits for its
driver, who sleeps
in the gray house near
the river; who has not
forgotten his run before
the sun ignites the sky; but this day
begins with Jesus in the river
of his soul, calling him to run with Him.

Sacrifice

Powerful prayer
is the food on my plate
that I choose to consume
not because it is delicious.
It is not.
Not because it is my favorite;
it is not.
I cannot even say it is tolerable.
I take each bite for the chef who made it;
because he spent himself
for me and for the others at the table,
preparing his signature meal,
the masterpiece he would gladly present
to Papa Francesco!

It sits inside me now,
seemingly immobile.
The memory of its awful taste
remains with me.
My body begs for abstinence in the future.
Jesus merely smiles,
and tells me this too shall pass.

Separation

You
left me
with questions
I can't answer.
I ask the Father,
but I can't decipher
His silence. Fear multiplies,
and I become a fraying rope:
a fragile prayer that won't hold me long;
but God holds me long, never letting go.

Snow Bird

I was tempted
to stop and photograph her
as she two-stepped atop the snow bank
on the side of the road;

but I was preempted
by the thought of her
ending her dance abruptly,
because of my intrusion.

I could not be so rude
to one whose gaiety in snow
was rare and welcome and
deepened with her colors
of an autumn too distant to recall.

Russet and red was her display,
like Anthony and Aaron,
inseparable since conception,
buddies on a mission to rewrite rules.

Chickens rewrite rules.
Even during an insistent winter
of persistent snow,
chickens still cross the road
at the Say of God Almighty,

Whose Mercy never fails chickens
or us in need of the other side.

Steps

I noticed her:
pink hoodie, brown pants,
parked on the second step;
gray hair loose, lightly brushed,
not long from the chair beside her bed,
not long from the sidewalk in front of the
church;
staring at the doors, locked until the priest
arrived;
but she wouldn't be there to see him,
to talk with him about Annie and Pete.
Talking wouldn't bring them back.
Sitting might give her patience
to wait upon the Lord God;
to listen as the deep silence
showed her the way to Him,
the unmarked, dirt road she'd avoided,
even in the messiness of her misery;
but He was relentlessly gentle and patient
in His pursuit.
He had known her before she knew herself,
showing her that she didn't know herself at all.
She didn't know that she needed Him,
more than she needed Annie and Pete.
He showed her that they were with Him,

praying for peace in her soul and trust in her
heart;
and courage to wait for the priest
who could show her the steps to Heaven.

Stranger

He was making conversation
as we waited for our flights
to our separate destinations.

He asked a simple question.
I answered. He was stunned,
turned away without another word.

Apparently, I wasn't she
whom he'd imagined I'd be,
another mother with a child or three:
his loss,
for not listening longer
to my story in the making.

Years have passed, and still I
have never given birth, have never adopted.
I think of him and wonder if he
has ever met another like me.
I think not.

If he had listened, he would
have heard the commonalities in our stories:
that we have the same Father God,

that He gives us each the job that only we can
do,
that we grow in relationship with Him,
and with each other,
because of our varied tasks.

In Heaven,
when he and I speak again,
he will know this and have no regrets;
because our stories wait to be told and heard
in the cellars of our souls.

Suffering

Not a pretty prayer,
this constant tribulation:
God Almighty, is this REALLY necessary!?

Not a pretty prayer,
this constant tribulation:
Jesus, please help me!

Not a pretty prayer,
this constant tribulation:
Holy Spirit, show up!

These splinters from The Cross always find me.

Rewind me
to that moment before my birth on this earth,
when You were all I knew,
when trust was always new,
when I allowed You to steer me true.

Please! Show me Your Face
in every moment, every place.
Erase the deeds that drive me
into the abyss of emptiness;

where I imagine I am free,
when in truth I am lost
unable to see the cost
of my stupidity.

Help me Lord now!
Let this not be the bough
that breaks my soul
as if it were a Dresden bowl
senselessly deployed against a cinder block
wall,
as if my destruction could stall
the endless torrent of Your amazing grace.

Lord God, I know that I must run this race;
but Lord, not without You!
Please! Never without You!

Sumptuous!

An extraordinary cake
isn't easy to make,
and delicious cookies
are not for rookies.
Both require a desire
beyond the self;
not a notion from a yellowed book on a dusty
shelf,
but a motion from the ocean of God.
Do you think it odd,
that God would care
about a baking dare?
Remember, He's our Dad
and He's always glad
to cook with us
and look with us
into every detail;
especially those that impale
our fragile hearts.
God removes the darts,
and heals us
and seals us in His grace.
He longs for us to see His Face!

Cakes and cookies will lose their appeal,
when He opens our eyes to His most sumptuous
Meal!

Taken

Jesus,
You smiled at me
as if my plunge into the deep
had been for an afternoon swim
on a day too hot to bear.
In my thrashing, You reached for me,
and I for You.
You gave me no reprimand.
You simply drew me close to You,
and I knew I was home;
not for eternity,
but for the duration of the necessary
trials that show me Your Face.
You will not take my trials from me.
You will take me from me,
allowing me to take You
from the dot in my mind
into the entirety of my heart.

The Last Pew

Some arrive early to claim a space,
a pew place in the church
far from His altar,
from His priest
and from Himself;
but Jesus does not limit Himself
to His Eucharistic Self.
He is as present on His altar
as He is in every pew,
in every season,
in every heart.
He waits for us to notice Him,
to repose in Him
when even the last pew is full,
and the temptation for late comers
is departure post haste,
rather than hastening to Him;
but God's presence and His pursuit
are irresistible and unrelenting.
Even our NO!
will in no way
defile, diminish or delete
the perfection, the constancy and the complete
extravagance of His extraordinary love.
He is beyond our wretched blindness.
Would that we would trust Him,

shake the dust of our indifference to Him;
allow trust to ignite us,
invite us to live beyond the limit of our thought,
to pursue that which we ought;
because He who is perfect and holy in every
deed,
is all we ever need.

Tiny Fire

On a chilly, dripping night in early spring,
after the doorbell had finally ceased its ring,
we sat staring at the stones and the fire,
finding much in them to contemplate and
admire.

Silent in the wall for years,
they'd heard, but said nothing about our fears;
neither unexpected nor rare,
still we appreciated their
presence, like napping pheasants,
keeping us warm by absorbing the heat
letting us feel it in our feet
usually the last to lose the chill
making them susceptible to every ill
that deigns to test
the tenor of our rest.

But when we focus on the Christ,
we're immune to any heist.
Whatever He allows, we gladly take;
for He does all for our sake,
for His Kingdom on high
far beyond our earthly sky;

deep in the heart of mystery
written in holy history:
God is our eternal now
always showing us how
to live Heaven all the time,
not just for the sake of a tiny rhyme.

Traveler

No
fanfare
for this stroll
out the side door
rarely used by the
daily knitters, sitters
and TV quitters who knew
all the soaps by heart. Impatient
for the Lord's knock on her door, she leaves,
knowing not how, but that she must find Him.

Undone

On trial
for crimes He did not commit,
He answered when questioned;
but they were not convinced
by His words.
They were not convinced
by His Word.

In trials,
for the removal of grime,
I must submit;
but I complain,
convinced I'm not to blame
for my terse words
and worst behavior.
I resist.
My trials persist.

James
insists on the employment of joy
in the encounter with trials.
Trials are necessary, he says;
for faith,
for perseverance,
for perfection,
for completeness.

He should know.
He's where I want to be,
when I'm done.

Unrelenting

Most
thought her foolish to meet his plane,
to agree to yet another encounter.
He had done enough,
they reasoned.
Her humiliation was an ever rising
pile of maggots
that they would refuse to endure.
Why would she?

Some
understood that her friendship
with his mother was not
a relationship she could
dismiss as quickly as he
had dismissed her.
He had never understood
the bond between his mother and his wife.
Perhaps it was jealousy that pushed him
into affairs and divorce and bottles
that never served him
what he needed.

One
chose to sacrifice her life for him,
as One had offered His life for her.
She knew,
as she knelt beside what remained
of his flesh,
that God Almighty had heard her prayer;
that unimaginable Mercy
had healed his wounded soul,
his broken heart;
and delivered him
into everlasting gladness.

Walker

Sometimes,
words are like birds
congregating on the frozen Cocheco;
chattering on about the gathering
of fish, plentiful and plump,
in the Atlantic.
I pen them to the page
and they begin to age
like fine wine
in the depths of a cellar.

But today,
the river is quiet ice,
and the wind has forgotten
how to howl.
In the silent solitude of my thoughts,
I recall the cry of the seagull in flight,
and I make my way to the sea.
I see Him in the distance,
walking on the water toward me.
I smile at His sure and certain steps,
expecting nothing less from His vast creature
than absolute obedience to the Word.
Jesus stops and smiles,
instructing me to join Him;
but I become the ice I left behind,

unable to allow His grace to flower
and blossom in me.

He waits.

Water

Endlessly rushing,
meets jagged rocks, silencing
their need to damage.

Writer's Camp

A substantial, flat sheet
would not limit itself
to covering the two corners
of a mattress at the foot of a bed.
It would flow to the floor
from every corner and side,
insuring its occupant
sufficient excess to pitch a tent
in the night light of a flashlight
held to the page that cannot rest
until each circumstance exhales
from the graveyard of the heart,
and appears as word
in black ink
on white paper without lines;
because lines limit,
and limits have
no part of God Who knows
each word, each circumstance;
each sin that holds me captive,
that keeps me
from His mercy,
His healing:
His unlined Heart.

About the Author

Photo by Sister Mary Joseph

Sister Mary Grace has made her first profession with the Roman Catholic community of the Daughters of Mary, Mother of Healing Love. She is grateful for God's innumerable gifts, including poetry, photography, and mercy -- especially in this extraordinary Jubilee Year of Mercy. Her first book of poetry, "Nothing To Do, But Pray," was published in 2014.